Post breakapocalyptic attempts at dealing

Victoria Valenzuela

BookLeaf Publishing

Presentation by *BookLeaf Publishing*

Web: www.bookleafpub.com

E-mail: info@bookleafpub.com

ISBN: 9789357213608

First edition 2023

Apartment

She is told-- her heart is an apartment complex.
Divvied up into equal spaces for all.
They say it like it's a bad thing,
But how could it be bad to love?
"You can't mean it"
She's told every time she says I love you-
She is told she says it too much,
It loses its meaning.
How can it if it's true?
She loves them all, each and every one,
with all her heart and soul.
She never lied about that.
All she regrets is that
there isn't enough
time in the world
to give them all that they deserve.
They say she is an apartment complex
like it's a bad thing.

Pendulum

I swing like a pendulum
Calculated arcs
Each extreme closer than I would like to admit
I realize that Reality lies in neither.
At rest is a home I will never visit.
The good memories overshadow the bad
And that is how I end up back in your arms.
So now I hold my point at the other extreme.
There are no good moments between us.
Every memory must be poisoned.
I alter my take on them.
The bad memories overshadow the good.
Staying safe.

Bookmark

The girl is a bookmark
Holding place and holding space
For something that is not hers

She is a bookmark
Holding place and holding space
Marking the dull chapter you chose
To end your night at

She is a bookmark
Holding place and holding space
Between chapter 5's character building
heartbreak
And "happily ever after, the end"

The girl is a bookmark
Holding place and holding space
But never having a story of her own
No sweet ending in sight

Devolution

The girl has evolved.
The girl has devolved
The girl is no longer a bookmark.
The girl is a footnote.
Occasionally used,
Typically hardly glanced at.
Less useful than the bookmark,
Technically necessary.

The girl has evolved.
The girl has devolved.
The girl is no longer a footnote.
The girl is the bibliography.
Once again, technically she has to exist.
But would it really matter if she didn't?

Quartz

In the wee hours of the night,
The world stays still.
Time freezes as I hold you,
High upon this hill.

I wrap you around me,
Shroud myself in your love.
I wrap you around me,
Watch the moon up above.

Your Caress repairs my cracks,
Fills in the missing parts.
My original is dull ceramic.
But you? Yours is glittering quartz.

On this hill we stay all night,
Neither moves, speaks or cries.
Early dawn breaking bright
Our entwined material solidifies.

Broken Moments

As I see the concrete
Rushing to meet my face
As I am falling
From the sky
As I feel my heart
stop Pounding
I realize this:
I realize why.

What led me here.
What caused this.
All were no more-
No less than omens.
The shattered glass

Lining my path.
leading me here:
All the broken moments

And in that instant
All that broken past
Was perfectly rearranged.
Finally, at last.

Decisions

As I tell a story of how
I punched a guy who tried to kiss me
You say 'wow, that's good.
What happened to you?"
I look back at the days
I chose to bite my tongue
It hurt less than the hit
I would take from arguing.
I look back at the days when
I lay motionless underneath him,
Visualizing I was anywhere else.
It didn't feel good,
but at least this didn't hurt (yet).
I look back at all the times
I swallowed my pride instead of my blood.
I look back at all of the times
I sacrificed my self worth
            to preserve my life.
"Everything happened."

Regrets

My life today tastes
Of puke and regrets.
Every decision I've made so far,
Has never been up to par.
I can handle what life has given,
I know this is where I have driven.

I've never known pain like this,
Fuck "ignorance is bliss."
Betrayal of the worst kind,
Go ahead, break my mind.
Kick me when I am down,
Leave me alone to drown.

It doesn't mater anymore,
Leave all expectations at the door.
I said my philosophy was tit for tat,
Now its too late to go back.

Trapped

I am so tired of inhabiting
this body that is stuck
in this web of emotions.
They called me spider-
long ago.
But spider I no longer am.
As I get caught in the sticky fibers
Surrounding my many legs
Spider I was-
When in control of my surroundings.
Now I struggle against all that I am
Spider I was-
When I had others ensnared,
Wrapped up as my nourishment.
These long long legs-
Made to keep me stable
Have now become the reason I am trapped.

Sharp

I don't trust you to stay
I don't expect you to love me
I don't need you to come back
But after the nights we spend together
The contrast of my cloudy sky
 Is set all the way up.
Sharp Relief.
And I swear to all he gods
I saw a sliver of a rainbow
on my way out.

Never change

Broken promises
Year after year
Broken hearts
Life after life
Anything expected
Soon forgotten
          A vow to change
Followed by
          When did I say that?
Heart break.
Hopelessness.
Dark vast abyss
In the end
You expect me to change
Every aspect of my
Personality
Yet you cannot change
A single facet of your
Vocabulary

My Demons

I can feel it,
Feel them.
Slouching and swaying
To an unheard tune.
Moving and rotating
Hatred in motion.
I feel them awaken.
A gutteral growl-
Hunger deep in their burning eyes.
I hear them.
Rattling and clanking
The chains that hold them.
They're loose and coming-
My demons are coming for me.

Ocean Life

I move too fast they say
This is a disaster waiting to happen
I am a frightened octopus
Darting from one hurt to the next
I am a startled eel
Refusing to leave my dark cave
I am a small starfish
Regrowing what has been taken
I do all this and more for the sake-
The sake of feeling alive
I play
I hurt
I kill myself
over and over
Just to exist

You Are Mine

You are mine for now-
Now, as we press our bodies together.
Now, as we try desperately to inhabit the same space.

You are mine tonight-
As we drink far too much.
As we let our guards down.
As we finally talk about truths.

In this moment-
We belong together.
No one can stop us.
Nothing outside matters.

Tomorrow you may leave me-
Wash me off and get dressed
In your walls and barricades.

Tomorrow we will go back to normal-
But tonight?
Hold me tight and drink from my soul...
I am yours.

The Untouchable

There are days I feel as though
I can do it all.
There isn't a thing
Beyond my grasp.

Reality hits.
I realize that there
will never be enough of me
To make you mine.

I see you as the stars-
Light years away
You float high above
Ever oblivious.

As I am stuck on this
Spinning ball of dirt.
Never able to feel your warmth.

Wolf

I apologize to that one
who now wants to hold my delicate heart,
I apologize if it turns to ashes before your eyes.
I apologize if my hugs feel like a thorn bush.
I apologize if my kisses are antifreeze.
I apologize for flinching,
          for overthinking, for every time I revert.
I apologize for talking about this so much.

It must be tiring to listen to the same song again.

And I thank you.
For being so willing to burn up with me
as I walk through the fires of my memory.
For being the concrete barriers I drive my car
into
when my brain turns into squirming maggots
that can only repeat the same thought.
For learning to crush those maggots
when you assure me that my life is changing,
that this time I am enough.
For being able to soothe my trembling bones
as I begin to recover my own flesh from the
mouth
of the hungry wolf.
For not being another wolf.

Writing Prompt

You are just another
writing prompt.
A sad story, begging
To be told.
You are the staples holding
my book together.
Coiled up ink
Replacing my veins.
You are just another
Writing prompt

Another reason to be up
At 3 A.M.

Slime

I have thought of myself as naive.
It hurt less than being stupid.
But even in my darkness I could see
I could see through those lies.

Like plastic wrap keeping
homemade slime contained.
My mother wrote with the kitchen Sharpie
"God kows all, it is his will"
And left this bag of goop in my hands.

Then there was the violation, the desectration
Once. And again. And Again.
Each new pain left a hole
In this slippery bag.

Death. Fights. Depression.
The slime leaks from the bag
onto my arms.
Onto the red patterned floor.
So. Much. Death.
And fear?
Suicidal thoughts.

The bag is emptier than not.
You return, angry at the empty bag.
"I gave you what you needed,
this was EVERYTHING"
I leave, but the slime has stained me.
No matter what I do, the traces remain.

Time Travelling

As I lie beneath your body
A question is asked.
Suddenly my reality disintegrates.
And I am time travelling.

There is a quick and sudden reminder that
Everything within me has been destroyed.

This body is not a sunken ship
A beautiful display of destruction.

This body is not an ashen forest
A tragic loss of life and scenery

This body is a crumbling city.
My mind a store with only rotten merchandise,
Nothing of use.
The 7/11 is out of gasoline
to power through my veins.
My heart is all the dead and decayed flesh
on which feral animals feast.

There is no beauty here.
Only the slow descent into nothing.

Pumpkin

My best friend says that I am a peanut.
But I think that he is wrong.
I am a pumpkin.
But not in the way
That you call a loved one or
A small child pun'kin
With love and affection
and the best of intentions.

No, I am a pumpkin in the sense of their use.
Once.
Open them up
Tear out their insides
Take away their flesh
            Everything of use
It is nourishment
Doesnt matter for who.
And the rest?
The empty shell is left to rot.
My skin-- wilting and dying out in the sun.

Sometimes its even fun
Playing with the carcass
Cutting it up
            Pretty little shapes

But nonetheless they are playing
with a dead thing.

Deepwater Horizon

He was supposed to be a blessing
That became a curse.
This human was my Deepwater Horizon
We were excited to see his existence.
Proud of the engineering feat.
Awed at the level of productivity.

Then it began.

The breakage which could not be repaired.
The slimy ooze that spilled from within.
Affecting all those around you.
Destruction.
Death, within and without.
It has been years and still the damage remains.

www.ingramcontent.com/pod-product-compliance
Lightning Source LLC
Chambersburg PA
CBHW051722130826
49812CB00034B/1297
* 9 7 8 9 3 5 7 2 1 3 6 0 8 *